see at a glance that he was a man who had roughed it on the veld.
He held out his hand and remarked " Well how are things down
South?" I replied " How do you know that I come from the south?"
He laughed and remarked " It is only people from the south you would
see walking about here without a coat on." " Right," I said, " I
have not worn a coat for months, come in and have a drink." I found
that it was a hotel run by a Greek, and that he was the only guest
staying there. I do not think that there were more than a dozen
white men living in Mombasa in those days. As we sat down I
could see that he had been drinking very heavily, and he remarked
" You are just the man I have been looking for, you are going with
me on my expedition to Uganda." I replied " Right," when do we
start? " He replied " As soon as we can, we will have to get busy
to-morrow, the Sudanese troops have mutinied in Uganda, and have
shot a number of their officers. They are a bad lot so we must get
away as soon as possible.'

What luck I thought, I was already on the march again to
another war, just as if it had all been arranged for my special benefit.
As we were short of porters I persuaded him to take some donkey
waggons. They were some of the first on that road. Little did I
dream of the trouble I was piling up for myself when I suggested
donkey waggons, as I am sure that everyone will agree who has ever
trekked in rainy weather on a bad road across the African veld or got
stuck in a drift with the river coming down. It is a job in which
you have to control your temper, and your language as well. I remember trying to pass a military camp early one morning when all
my donkeys got mixed up with the tent ropes. I was not surprised
when I saw a man rush out of his tent in his pyjamas, but got a
shock when he vigorously started shaking me by the hand, and at
the same time remarked " Allow me to congratulate you on your
fluent flow of language. I am a Sergeant Major, and all the years
that I have served in the army I have never heard anything to equal
it." You may bet I felt highly elated, as it was the first time that
I had ever been praised by a Sergeant Major.

About a week later we found ourselves camping at the railhead
of the Uganda Railway, which was in course of construction to stop
the slave trade, or at least so it was said. Railhead then, was about
one hundred miles from the coast. From there the caravan road
wound its way, through one of the wildest parts of Africa, a country
full of wild game and still wilder men. The lions were devouring by
the dozen the Indian coolies who were engaged in building the railway, and white men also. One white man was taken out of his tent
in front of his wife by one of these man-eaters. Another was taken
bodily out of a railway carriage, the lion went in at the door and
pushed through the window with the man. The Masai were holding
up caravans and murdering the porters. One white man had his
caravan wiped out with about a thousand men, including himself.
The wild and savage Kikuyu into whose country no one dare enter,
also took their toll of the caravans that skirted the borders of their
country, and at one time had even gone as far as to capture a British

rort. The Nandi natives had murdered the porters who were carrying a steel boat, the " Sir William Mackinnon," up to Lake Victoria Nyanza, and used the material for making spears and arrow heads. The Sudanese troops had mutinied and shot their officers. There was very little protection for travellers along that historic road, except for a few small forts about a hundred miles apart garrisoned with one or two white officers, and about thirty to forty black soldiers.

This is just a rough outline of how I found the country I was about to enter. Those who only know the Kikuyu people as they are to-day may find some difficulty in crediting many of the statements I shall make as to their character and reputation at the time when I spent some three or four very lively years among them, but a short quotation from the late Sir Gerald Portal's book on the " British Mission to Uganda in 1893," dealing with the race as they were then, and which accurately describes them as I found them five years later, may help the doubting ones to a closer realisation of the facts. Describing the British East Africa Company's station, Fort Smith, in the Kikuyu country, Sir Gerald says : " The Kikuyu tribes were practically holding the Company's station in a state of siege " Later on he says . " We left the open plain and plunged into the darkness of a dense belt of forest, which forms the natural boundary of the regions inhabited by the treacherous, cunning, and usually hostile people of the Kikuyu Warned by the state of affairs which we had heard was prevailing at the Company's fort in this district, we were careful to keep all our people together, every man within a couple of paces of his neighbour. One European marched in front, one in the rear, and one in the middle of the long line The Wa-Kikuyu, as we knew, very seldom or never show themselves and run at the risk of a fight in the open, but he like snakes in the long grass, or in some dense bush within a few yards of the line of march, watching for a gap in the ranks, or for some incautious porter to stray away, or loiter a few yards behind; even then not a sound is heard, a scarcely perceptible ' twang ' of a small bow, the almost inaudible whizz ' of a little poisoned arrow for a dozen yards through the air, a slight puncture in the arm, throat, or chest, followed, almost inevitably, by death Another favourite trick of the Wa-Kikuyu is to plant poisoned skewers in the path, set at an angle of about forty-five degrees, pointing towards the direction from which the stranger is expected. If the path is much overgrown or hidden by the growth of the grass, these stakes are of much greater length and so pointed that they would pierce the stomach of anyone advancing towards them Keeping a sharp lookout for these delicate attentions, our progress was inevitably slow, but at length we arrived without further adventure at the strong stockade, ditch, brick houses, and well guarded stores known as Fort Smith in Kikuyu, above which was floating the Company's flag Outside the Fort itself the state of affairs was not so pleasant to contemplate. We were surrounded day and night by a complete ring of hostile Wa-Kikuyu, hidden in the long grass and bushes, and for anyone to wander alone for more than two hundred yards from the stockade was almost certain death

" On the morning of our arrival, a porter of Martin's caravan who had strayed down to the long grass at the foot of the little hill on which the station is built, was speared through the back and killed within 250 paces of our tents. A short time before, eight soldiers in the Company's service who were foraging for food—probably in an illicit manner—were all massacred in a neighbouring village; and a day or two before our arrival the natives had even had the temerity to try to set fire to the fort itself at night. It will, however, be a matter of time and difficulty requiring great tact, patience, and firmness, to induce these Wa-Kikuyu to have confidence in Europeans, and to discontinue their practice of spearing or otherwise murdering any defenceless Swahili porter whom they may find straying away by himself."

Long before I went to their country I remember being told by an African traveller of great renown that the only way in which to deal with the Kikuyu people, whether singly or in masses, was to " shoot at sight." The " Martin " mentioned by Sir Gerald Portal above was one of the pioneers of British East Africa. He was a Maltese sailor, who came to this country with Joseph Thompson, and was the first white man to venture among the Masai. Another traveller, Mr. G. F. Scott Elliott, speaking of the Kikuyu in his book, " A Naturalist in Mid Africa," says: " They are only too anxious to spear a lagging porter." He also describes the murder by these people of forty-nine out of fifty men, comprising an Arab or Swahili trading caravan. Later on I was destined to be the first white man to live amongst this pleasant people, enter into their daily life, and bring them into something like close touch with European civilisation.

In January, 1898, I said " goodbye " to my partner at railhead and I never met him again. I continued my trek with my small donkey convoy, and about 100 porters to Uganda. It was arranged that as soon as I got loads delivered I was to send the receipt down to my partner by special runner, so that he could draw the money and fit out a big expedition for the Lake Rudolph district.

A few days later I was trekking across the Athi plains. All the way right up to Nairobi they were covered with game and so tame that I felt ashamed to shoot them when I required meat for my boys. They would stand and look at the waggons in wonderment. But, not so the lions. I had no end of trouble with them, especially when travelling at night by moonlight; I could easily tell when they were about as my donkeys would increase their pace and get into a run if the road happened to be level. Finally I arrived at Nairobi River. Little did I dream then that I should live to see in that swamp area a big city arise with its 100,000 inhabitants and become the capital of Kenya Colony. All I saw there was plenty of game on the plains and a couple of rhino disporting themselves in the swamp. The next day after penetrating a small forest I found myself on the border of the Kikuyu country. What a change, after crossing tireless plains with nothing but wild game and now to come upon this contrast. I saw one of the most beautiful parts of Africa, fertile soil, covered with cultivation, and here and there small stockaded villages with cattle and goats quietly grazing. I was warned to be careful when I reached the Kikuyu country and keep a good guard as they had a very bad name, being very treacherous and not to be trusted in any way.

I delivered all my loads in Uganda, sent the special runner with the receipt to my partner down at the coast, then followed myself with the donkey waggons. On arriving at railhead I was informed that my partner had already left with a big safari of rifles and ammunition, but as no one could tell me where he had disappeared to I took a contract myself and proceeded for another trip to Uganda with the donkey waggons, but this trip turned out an utter failure as all my donkeys died except one They must have got fly bitten at railhead, so I found myself stuck, far from anywhere, on the African veld, with one donkey and three boys It was impossible to take the waggons back without donkeys, so taking the lid off one of the food boxes I painted thereon with waggon grease, "Dead Donkey Camp," and having stuck this up I left the waggons and never saw them again Having packed my sole remaining donkey with my food and cooking pots on one side and my bedding on the other, I started and trekked back to the Government Fort at Naivasha

Now to review the position I stood in, here I was stranded on the veld, in one of the wildest parts of Africa, with very little food, three natives, one donkey with blankets on one side and a few cooking pots on the other, one rifle and about 50 rounds of ammunition. Although I had lost all my waggons I had not lost my desire for further adventure and the opportunity of getting away into some hitherto unexpected part of the country I found food was wanted at the Government Stations at Naivasha, as well as for the surveying parties on the line of the Uganda Railway, and it worth a rupee a pound Everybody knew that the Kikuyu country was full of food, but any parties that had gone to buy supplies had always been killed by the natives, and as a matter of fact news had just come through that a party who were out buying food had all been wiped out only a few miles from Fort Smith I found out that I could get into the Kikuyu country from Naivasha by going north over the Kinangop plains through the Masai country and then over the Aberdare Range, the highest peak of which is about 12,000 feet above sea level).

At last having arranged my small safari which consisted of seven natives, some knowing the Kikuyu language (by this time I had learnt the Swahili language), I set out to explore the unknown I had only got about five miles on my journey when I was overtaken by a white Sergeant with some native soldiers and taken back to Naivasha Government Station, there I was introduced to the Officer in Charge, and asked if I was trying to commit suicide He said he would not think of going there himself with less than one machine gun and thirty rifles and if he let me go I was certain to be killed and he would then be held responsible for allowing me to leave the district. I tried him with every argument I could think of to let me go, but he was adamant On thinking back now I see that he was quite right You may be sure that I felt disappointed but not discouraged

for I felt somehow that I would pull through alright. Something
within me was egging me on, if I was to be killed the very
next day, nothing would stop me now. Had I not beaten my way
up there, all the way from the south, for this very thing, a new
country, which had never been explored? Besides, had I not helped
to take over Matabeleland, what would my old pioneer friends of the
camp fires think about me if I failed. I fancied I could hear them
say, " Got the wind up, no guts."

To get beyond the jurisdiction of the official at Naivasha, I
trekked off to the Kedong Valley, which forms a portion of the great
rift, a depression which seems to divide the Continent of Africa east
from west and which in those days was the boundary between British
East Africa and Uganda. From there I duly set out for my land
of promise, entering the Kinangop plain—the Masai grazing ground,
a fine stretch of open country.

That night I camped on the edge of the bamboo forest at about
8,000 feet altitude, after passing through herds of game intermingled
with Masai cattle, sheep and goats. I had no trouble with the Masai
as I had Masai boys on my safari. The Masai are not so treacherous
at the Kikuyu, they will warn you that they are going to attack,
whereas the Kikuyu will try and stab you in the back.

The next morning we trekked over the mountain after finding
an old elephant track, forcing our way through the bamboos which
the elephants had broken down, and trees that had fallen across
the track. On we went, bamboos, nothing but bamboos. At last we
reached the top, an altitude of about 12,000 feet, down we went, the
other side, making better headway. It was almost dark when we
camped for the night still in the bamboo forest. Continuing our
journey, the next morning we fell in with some Kikuyu natives, they
would not stop to talk to us, but off they went, shouting their war
cry, ' Hue,he-ee." Many and many a time was I to hear this
inspiring cry, which was always used in times of danger or war,
shouted from village to village and hill to hill.

I had heard someone cutting wood in the forest off our road,
and news of our coming had spread. At the first sight of us the
natives had started runnig away, but we soon heard their war cry
being taken up from hill to hill round about, and could catch occa-
sional glimpses of the natives themselves as they gathered in force
towards the village. They were certainly a wild looking lot, with
bodies smeared all over with grease and red clay, with in some cases,
a kind of whitewash, in which patterns were drawn according to the
fancy of the individual. Fastened to the leg was a rattle, with an
iron ball inside, which, as they moved about, made a noise very much
like a railway train. Many of them wore wonderful head-dresses,
made of the skin of the colobus monkey and all were armed with
spears and shields.

In a short time quite five hundred warriors, fully armed, were
drawn up outside the village, and getting within speaking distance,
I told my Masai interpreter to tell them that I had come to see the
chief of the district.

Never having seen a white man before, they regarded me with something like awe, being puzzled at my appearance, and were at a loss how to act. The fact that I had ventured to come there alone was, in itself, quite enough to surprise and astonish them, and noting the impression I had made, I knew that if I was to succeed with them I must keep up an attitude of fearlessness.

After my interpreter had spoken, a guide came forward to conduct me to the chief whose name was Karuri. Accompanying the guide to the chief's kraal, I was met by Karuri, who demanded to know what I wanted.

It was a strange meeting, and one which was to have great consequences for both of us. As the time went on Karuri was to become my friend and right-hand supporter, while I, in turn was to have an influence over him and his people which was to raise him to the position of a great chief and myself to supreme power in the country.

Through my interpreter I explained my mission. I said that I had come to see his country and was anxious to trade with him and to buy food.

He then questioned me as to the force I had brought with me; to which I replied that, as my mission was a peaceable one, I had left most of my guns in the forest to avoid trouble, but that if he harmed me, my people would come and make war on him.

This pardonable untruth seemed to make the desired impression on him, and I gave him a present of cloth, which he accepted with every appearance of pleasure. After this his manner became more friendly, and when I signified my intention of making a long stay in his country he readily agreed that his men should build a hut for me.

His people still regarded me suspiciously, but obeyed my orders when I told them to fetch wood and set about the building of the hut, under my instructions. They also brought me a sheep and some flour and sweet potatoes, and as I had by this time got a fire going, I had a good meal cooked for myself and my men, the Kikuyu all the time looking on with much interest.

In the meanwhile I had been looking round and taking stock of the neighbourhood, and a wilder scene it would be hard to imagine. The Kikuyu country is a succession of small hills separated by deep valleys, lined with water courses fed from the higher country. The hills are beautifully wooded, except where the trees have been cleared away to get patches of ground for the cultivation of crops.

The village, which was situated on the high ground in a large clearing in the forest, consisted of a cluster of round huts, surrounded by a high thorn fence or boma, high enough and thick enough to make any attempt at forcing an entrance by a force unprovided with good axes a matter of great difficulty. The entrance through the boma was by means of a narrow tunnel made of large slabs of wood, sunk deeply in the ground, with the tops interlocking at such an angle that anyone wishing to enter had to crawl through it on hands and knees. The walls of the huts were made of huge slabs of wood, fashioned out of large trees by the simple process of cutting portions off the trunk until it was reduced to the required thickness. These slabs were placed upright in the ground, close together in the form of a circle, and a thatched roof built up over them. By the side of the huts, which were built without any attempt at regularity, were smaller structures, with basket floors and grass roofs, which I found were used as granaries, or larders, in which to store the food.

The people who gathered round us while the meal was being got ready were a fierce-looking crowd. Everyone seemed to be discussing me, and, by the looks cast in my direction, debating whether, after all, they should not kill me. Not knowing what might happen, I kept my rifle near me and my bandolier in readiness in case of sudden attack.

After a time they became more inquisitive, and began to examine my clothes, which were something new to them, as they had never seen anything of the sort before. The boots puzzled them the most, as they appeared to think they were actually part of my feet, which they seemed to think were very curiously constructed. Some of them pushed their curiosity to the extent of wanting to examine my rifle, but this I refused to let out of my hand.

My interpreter said that they thought I was very foolish to come among them with only one rifle, so I told him to tell them that this gun was different from any that they had seen before and far more effective than those carried by Arab and Swahili traders. The gun, I explained, could kill six men with one shot and I told them that I would show them what it would do by firing at a tree. It happened to be the old Martini-Metford, so, putting in a solid cartridge, I chose a tree that I knew the bullet would go through and fired. They immediately rushed to see what damage had been done and when they found the hole where the bullet had entered and came out the other side, they were both considerably surprised and impressed. I assured them that that was nothing; if they would examine the side of the mountain beyond they would find that the bullet had gone right through that as well; I knew that only sheer bluff could bring me safely out of the position in which I had placed myself, and so made the best use of every opportunity that arose of impressing them.

Turning into my hut, I kept awake practically all night, fearing that some treachery might be attempted, but fell asleep at last, to be awakened early in the morning by an awful row of war-horns and men shouting and running about in every direction. By the time I had rubbed the sleep out of my eyes I saw a crowd of very excited natives rushing towards my hut and fully expected that I was in for a tough fight. However, far from intending to attack me, they had come to implore my help for themselves. It seemed that though Karuri, in his younger days, had been a powerful chief, his influence had waned as he grew older, and the tribe had been split up into clans, something like the Highlanders in the old days, in the absence of a chief sufficiently strong to keep the various sections in order, and they were continually indulging in petty wars among themselves. One of the neighbouring clans had heard of my arrival, and, objecting to the presence of any white man in the country, had promptly attacked Karuri's village, with the object of disposing of me once and for all, and a big fignt, in which a number of people had already been killed, was then in progress, and, looking out of my hut, I saw that a portion of the village was in flames. My duty was clear. These people had brought the trouble on themselves by befriending me, and the least I could do was to give them such help as I could Besides, I wished to remain in the country, and if they were worsted—even if I escaped with my life, which was very unlikely—I should have to get out and stay out, for some considerable time, at any rate. It did not take me long to make up my mind, and, seizing my rifle, I made for the scene of the fight, accompanied by a crowd of yelling savages, delighted at my decision. When I arrived the row was at its height, and the sight of the hand-to-hand conflict among the warriors, sur-rounded by the burning huts, was a stirring one. Seeing the reinforce-ments, headed by myself, coming up, the attackers began to waver, and when I fired a few shots with effect, finally turned and bolted. After pursuing them for some distance to make sure that they were completely shattered, the triumphant warriors returned to the vill.ge and made quite a hero of me, being convinced that their victory was entirely due to my help This incident was of the greatest value to me, as it fully established my reputation as a useful member of the community, and they became very friendly. I learned that they had a lot of trouble with this particular clan, who had frequently raided them, killing many of their men, and carrying off their cattle, and sometimes their women.

After this, Karuri came to ask me if I would stop in his country and I told him I would think about it I said that I had other work to do, but that if he would sell me flour and other foodstuffs I would come back to him I told him that the flour was for friends of mine, who were coming along the caravan road He said that he did not want any more white people in his country. I could stop as long as I liked myself, and his people would be my friends, but they did not mean to have any strangers I explained that though my friends were coming along the caravan road they had no intention or desire to enter the country This explanation seemed to satisfy him, and I told him that I would not decide at once about staying, but that when I had taken the flour to my friends I would come back, and talk matters over with them Then they asked what I had to give in exchange for the flour, and I produced a bottle of iodoform, some of which I had used on their wounds after the fight, with good effect They thought it was great medicine and all wanted some, and in exchange for a small quantity, wrapped in paper, would give from ten to twenty pounds of flour They looked upon me as a great medicine man When I found that I had about 200 loads of food, 60 lbs per load, the trouble was to find porters to carry it I finally succeeded in pressing a number of the people into my service and started off with my loads for the caravan road

On arriving on the caravan road I was lucky enough to fall in with some railway surveyors I was ahead of my safari when I met them and asked if they wanted to buy any food for their men They said they would buy all the food I could bring and would give me 30 rupees a load for it. When I told them that within a few hours I could let them have 200 loads of flour, they could hardly believe it, nor that I had been in the Kikuyu country with one rifle and come out alive. Thirty rupees is £2 per load, so I had made £400 on my first trip into the Kikuyu country.

I was able to buy a large quantity of trade goods, beads and cloth, from Arab traders going up to Uganda; my only trouble was that I could not get any rifles and ammunition. I knew that I would not be able to hang out in the Kikuyu country with only one rifle very long, and sooner or later I would get killed. Although the Government was starving for food, they would not help me in any way. All they would say was, " We do not want you to go out there, you are sure to get killed," and did their best to stop me.

Having made up my mind to stay in the Kikuyu country, I selected a site and got them to help me to build a house in the European style. While this was going on I used to have regular visits from the witch doctors. They seemed the most intelligent of the tribe and, seeing I did not interfere with their religion, most of them got very friendly with me. I was anxious to get to know all I could about these people, so I got the most influential of them to live near me. I had a very big grass shed built where we all met once a week. I used to kill a few sheep for them and let them have a beer drink, and in that way got to know them very well. As a matter of fact, I got to know them so well and their little games that if there was a smelling out, I knew the victim beforehand, just as they did. They proved themselves very useful to me and acted as my Scotland Yard. I got to know everything that was going on in the country, and learnt that an Arab safari with a lot of ivory and about 100 rifles had been wiped out near the slopes of Mount Kenya. That was about two long days' march away. If I could only get those rifles it would mean everything to me. It meant that I had to go about 50 miles through a thickly inhabited hostile country, and the people who had the rifles were a very hostile and war-like clan of the Kikuyu tribe. The very fact that they had wiped out a huge Arab safari of about 200 strong proved this. What chance did I stand, with just my one rifle? Nothing venture, nothing gained, kept repeating itself to me. Finally I made up my mind and selected 100 of my best men armed with spears and shields. I trained them a little with sticks and my one rifle, and we started off one dark night just after sunset, with the blessing of all the witch doctors, and a rainmaker to keep the rain away, as we had to sleep out in the bush. We did not want to get wet, and I may say right now that he kept his contract, for we never had a drop of rain. He was rewarded with one sheep for his work on our return. The expedition turned out a big success. We slept out in the bush the first day, after travelling all through the night, and the next day arrived at the hostile chief's village early in the morning before daybreak. When he woke up he found himself surrounded, and before he had time to realise what had happened, I had him covered with my rifle and ordered him to tell his people to bring

in all the rifles and ammunition of the murdered Arabs, and that
at the least sign of treachery, he would be a dead man

Out of the hundred rifles only thirty were of any use   With them
I armed thirty of the best men I could find, taking great trouble in
teaching them how to use them   After a time I was able to put the
squad. through the Manual exercises in English though it always
puzzled me to know how they understood what I wanted them to do

In the meanwhile I had been getting better acquainted with the
country, and found that the people lived in a constant state of civil
war.   Every day men came to me to have their wounds dressed, and
I heard of many being killed   As I have already said, the country was
very mountainous and each hill had its own chief, who lived in a
state of continual warfare with his neighbours.   No man was safe in
travelling about the country, except on certain days, when a sort of
general market was held, during the continuance of which a truce
seemed to exist, hostilities being resumed again as soon as it was over.

Karuri used to visit me nearly every day, and from him I learned
all about the country   Even he seemed to be afraid to go far from
his own village, and, as this state of affairs was very bad for my plans
of trading, I determined to do what I could towards reducing the
country to something like order   There was a good deal of fighting
going on and many of the friendly natives were being killed through
the hostility of the neighbouring chiefs and their people towards me.
They strongly resented my intrusion into the country, and any of the
natives known to be friendly to me, or wearing any of the cloth I had
given them, were immediately marked down for attack.

This sort of thing went on for some time, and they began to think
that, because I took no action against their enemies, I was afraid of
them   There were threats to kill me every day, and one night, after
some of the villages had been burned, and a lot of people killed, they
came to me and asked me to take their part, saying that they had
always been friendly towards me, and that was why these people were
making war on them and robbing them   I therefore sent a messenger
to the offending chief to say that if he did not return the property
which had been stolen, and pay compensation for the murders committed, I should have to go and compel them to do so   (The law
of the country is that for every man killed, a payment of one hundred
sheep shall be made, and for every woman, thirty sheep)   The chief
simply returned an insulting message to the effect that we were afraid
of him, and the next time he came he would kill me, too

A few days later I had a consultation with Karuri, and we came
to the conclusion that the only thing to be done was to go out and
fight the matter out with them, though I was strongly averse to
getting mixed up in any of their quarrels.   However, the matter was
settled for us, for while we were still negotiating for a peaceful settlement of the difficulty, our enemies came down in force one day and
attacked the village   They numbered altogether about five hundred
warriors, while we could only muster about three hundred   They
had been successful in previous raids because the people were scattered
about in a small number of villages, and could not muster in sufficient

force to beat them off, as they could always overwhelm a village and get away before any help could be brought to the spot. On this particular occasion, however, matters were a little different, as we had been expecting trouble, and had made arrangements to give them a warm reception if they should venture to come.

Our spies had been out for some time and kept us well informed as to what was going on, and gave us good warning as to when we might expect to be attacked.

As soon as the news of the approaching raid reached us, I mustered the fighting men and got ready to receive the invaders. We were soon made aware of thir approach by the sound of wild war-cries and savage yells, as well as by the flames of the burning villages, to which they had set fire as they came along, and, meeting with no opposition, no doubt they anticipated an easy victory.

By this time I had taught my people to hold themselves in check and act together, instead of each man fighting for his own hand. Waiting till they had got within easy striking distance, we poured in a volley of spears and arrows and I did service with my rifles. Following up the surprise caused by this unexpected reception, we were soon among them and engaged in a warm hand-to-hand fight, which lasted until we had beaten off the invaders and followed them right back into their country. The battle, which had started in the early morning, lasted until mid-day, and having administered severe punishment, we camped for the night in the enemy's territory.

We had had the good fortune to capture the enemy's chief, who was brought a prisoner into our camp, and the next morning I consulted with Karuri as to what was to be done with him, and it was decided to hold a shauri, or council, on the matter. Within a few days all the stolen property was restored to its original owners, causing much rejoicing among them, as they had, of course, never expected to see any of it again. Of course, I took precautions to see that no friction occurred during the process of re-transferring the recovered property, and having invited some of the chief men of both districts to my camp, we got on quite friendly terms.

Seeing them sitting, eating and drinking together amicably, it was difficult to imagine that they had been cutting one another's throats only a few days previously, but the Kikuyu, like many other African races, are remarkably changeable, and their temper can never be relied upon. As I learnt during my stay among them, they are both fickle and treacherous, and had it not been for my own people, I should have run great risk of being killed on several occasions, through trusting them too much.

I was very anxious to strengthen and maintain my friendship with these people and the surrounding clans, and, after some discussion on the matter, found that they had a ceremony, known as " Pigasangi," which was supposed to be mutually binding. If it could be arranged for me to go through this ceremony, there was every prospect of a lasting friendship being formed. This ceremony differs from that of blood-brotherhood, chiefly in that while blood-brotherhood establishes a friendly relationship with the individual, " Pigasangi " establishes it with the whole of the tribe or communities represented at the ceremony. After some days the assembled chiefs consented to take part in the ceremony, and accompanied by the natives who had always been friendly to me, and about fifteen of the old men of the district, I went to the chief's village to make the necessary arrangements.

When we arrived at the village the people were already waiting to receive us, and there were signs of great festivity. Word had been sent round to all the villages that the ceremony was to take place and, as it was looked upon as a great occasion for rejoicing, much dancing and beer-drinking were going on, and we were received with shouts of welcome and every sign of friendship A large clearing had been selected for the occasion—the Kikuyu, like many other savage tribes, always choosing an open space for their ceremonies, or discussions of importance ,as they were thus enabled to detect any would-be eavesdroppers before they could get near enough to overhear anything or to attempt any treachery Nearly all the native villages, I found. have a space set apart in the neighbourhood for the holding of their shauris and dances, etc

After a lot of superfluous oratory, the proceedings began with a black goat being brought in, with its feet tied up, and laid in the centre of the space The natives then grouped themselves in a circle, with the chiefs and orators in the centre Everybody taking part had previously been disarmed, and considering that there were over two thousand people present, it was remarkably how orderly and quiet the assembly was, everything being carried out without any hustling or disputing for right of place.

The native never speaks at any meeting of the tribe without a stick in his hand, and on the present occasion each speaker was provided with a number of sticks, having one for each subject of discussion ,the sticks being thrown on the ground by each alternatively as he went through his speech.

First one side and then the other stated the points of the agreement, which, of course, had been carefully discussed beforehand, so that there should be no chance of argument during the ceremony The main points were that there were to be no hostilities between the two clans in future, that they were to assist each other, and that neither should molest any white man coming through its country.

When all the sticks had been thrown down, they were collected and, being bound up in a bundle, were placed between the legs of the goat

The chief orator, whose stick was more like a club than the rest, then repeated the different conditions, at the end of each clause dealing the goat a heavy blow with his club, whilst repeating a formula to the effect that any one breaking the agreement should die like the goat By the time he had reached the last clause the animal was almost dead, and a particularly heavy blow dispatched it. After that no one dare touch the goat, which was regarded as sacred and I learned that this was the opportunity to obtain any confession from a native anyone suspected of wrong doing being asked to swear by the goat, when he would certainly tell the truth

The ceremony was now followed by more rejoicing and drinking of native beer.

This function considerably enlarged the area of friendly country, which now extended to the banks of one of the rivers which rises in the Aberdare Range, and flows in an easterly direction until it empties, as I afterwards found, into the Tana River. On the other hand, the fact that these people made friends with me had the effect of increasing the enmity of the other chiefs, who remained outside the agreement, and feared that the effect of it would be to lead more white men to come into the country.

May I beg the reader's indulgence to be allowed to digress a little to review my position before proceeding with my further adventures.

Here I was, quite a youngster in my early twenties, living by myself with a tribe of war-like savages, being the first white man they had ever seen, cut off from any outside help. I had thirty armed natives with rifles whom I had trained in their use. I also had at this time about a thousand trained men with spears and shields—I found it very necessary to have my natives better organised from a military point of view.

I knew that all my actions were very carefully watched and the white race would be judged by my behaviour ,so I made a point of never making a promise unless I was sure that I could carry it out, so that the natives could always rely on my word. I also trained myself never to show any sign of fear. I never attacked unless I was attacked first, or was forced to fight for my own life, or those of my people. No women or children were ever interfered with, hurt or molested. I never employed any strange natives, only natives of the country, all Wa-Kikuyu, and I never interfered with their laws or religion. If they were sick I gave them medicine, I introduced English potatoes into that part of the country, and also Black Wattle into Kenya Colony, getting the seed from Natal, South Africa. As a result, the whole of the Kikuyu country is now studded with Black Wattle plantations and must be keeping at least a dozen wattle bark factories going. There is no doubt that the natives and the country benefited greatly during the depression and locust infestation through my forethought.

The people in the immediate neighbourhood of the district, where I was living, now looked upon me as a great man. My advice had been good in their Councils, and I had succeeded in bringing about peace with their bitterest enemies. They also regarded me as a great medicine man, on the strength of a bottle of Eno's Fruit Salts, which they would come round in crowds to watch me drink, saying that the white man could drink boiling water; and they believed that I must have had a stomach like iron, and, being utterly ignorant, my friends were firmly convinced that it was impossible to kill me. The news of my presence spread all through the country, and many threats to kill me were uttered, it being reported that some of the hostile chiefs were banding together for that purpose.

In the meanwhile, at intervals of about ten days I would get the natives round about to come up to my house and dance. These dances were always held during the day-time. The Kikuyu are a very musical people, singing wherever they go and the warriors would come to the dances in a body, singing as they marched along, and keeping as perfect time and step as a regiment of trained soldiers. First of all, they would have a kind of march past, and then, falling out, would form a huge circle, with all the women and old men on the outside. First one warrior and then another would dart out from the circle and go through some weird evolutions. Every man was fully armed as if going on the war-path, and the movements took the form of a fierce fight with an imaginary foe. If the man was recognised as a great warrior he was violently applauded by the onlookers, and, encouraged by the signs of approbation, would work himself up into a perfect frenzy; but if he was a man who had not distinguished himself in any way, or was not popular among the tribesmen, his performance would be received in absolute silence.

One peculiar point that struck me about these people was the absence of any kind of musical instrument, even the usual drum. All their songs and dances were absolutely unaccompanied by any of the weird noises that, with most savage tribes, represent a musical accompaniment, and the only musical instrument that I ever knew of their making was a kind of whistle, something after the fashion of those made by boys at home from elder stems, and, I imagine, merely a toy; certainly I never saw them used by any but boys, and only on rare occasions by the boys themselves. I do not include among musical instruments the war-horn, an instrument usually made from the horn of a bullock, or a koodo, and which is simply used as an alarm.

A peculiar feature about the applause on these occasions was that it was confined to the women, the men considering it beneath their dignity to make any demonstration, whether of approval or contempt.

Although the women were not allowed to take any part in these dances themselves, they always appeared in full force as spectators, rigged out in their best go-to-meeting suits of skins, with their bodies plentifully smeared with grease, and wearing all their ornaments. When any favourite warrior had the floor, they expressed their approval by waving bunches of grass, and at the same time raising a musical chant of " lu-lu-lu-lu-lu." This chant, by the way, was the common form of welcome among them, as, when my safaris returned from any of our trips to Naivasha with food, the women would all turn out as we approached a village and greet us with a cry, which was taken up from hill to hill, as we went along.

They had some dances in which the women joined, and these were usually held at night round a big fire.

The Kikuyu seem to have more varieties of dances than any natives I know, and are, on the whole, a lighthearted race, singing all day long. They have a class of strolling minstrels, resembling more than anything the old troubadours of the Middle Ages. There were only five or six of these troups in the country altogether and, like the troubadours, they were a privileged class, travelling from place to place and extemporising songs about local events and people—not always without a strong tinge of sarcasm, which no one dared to resent. The Kikuyu were particularly clever in picking up the songs introduced by these troubadours, and a song that took the popular fancy would be taken up at its first hearing, and spread through the country with as much or even more rapidity than a music-hall ditty among the errand-boys of London, disappearing as rapidly when a new one came out. There was a further resemblance to the troubadours in the fact that they dressed in a fashion of their own, and wore a ring of small beads strapped round each ankle, and a single large one of iron fastened to each knee. They seemed to be free to pass where they pleased throughout the country, and I consequently encouraged them to visit me—which some of them would do every week—as they were able to keep me informed as to what was going on all over the country, so that I was able to meet any emergency that might arise.

The dances I arranged as a means of bringing the people together, so that I could talk to them afterwards and explain various things which at first they did not understand, such as the coming of the white man, who, I explained, did not come to raid their villages and make slaves of them, but wished to be friends in trade with them. The information I got from some of my visitors with regard to what was going on in the outlying districts was also very useful at times. For instance, about this time I found that a tribe whose district lay to the north of us was preparing to make a big raid through the whole country, as they did not want any white men there at all.

All this time the country was in a terrible state of unrest. Every night alarming messages were brought in that the people from the north were coming to attack us.

One night it would be the followers of Wagombi—a big chief living near Mount Kenia, who could muster two or three thousand fighting men—who were on the war-path. This chief had raided the whole of the country at one time or another, and though I had tried to get messengers through to him, they were always murdered.

Another night it would be the people of Tato who were coming down on us. All this time food was being collected and brought in, and I was anxious to explore the country still further, but was afraid to leave on account of these rumours of threatened attacks. If I had gone away I should have had to take the best of the people with me, and I knew that during my absence the hostile tribes would come down on the district, burn the place out and kill everyone who was left. Besides all the people urged me to stay with them and not to go away just yet.

I had taken the precaution of placing outposts to give us due warning of any attack, which I expected would take place, if it did come, early in the morning, just before daylight, this being the usual time for an attack, and for this reason the Kikuyu would not keep fowls lest the crowing of the cocks towards dawn should betray their villages—which are always hidden away in the bush—to the enemy.

This practice of delivering their attack just before dawn prevails among savage tribes pretty well all over the world, and I think that the main reasons which led to this time being chosen are, firstly, that the night offers the best opportunity of gradually bringing the force up into such a position that the enemy are surrounded before they can discover the movement which is in progress, and secondly, that it is the hour at which vitality is at its lowest and, consequently, the desire for rest and sleep has greater power over the body, and the force attacked is likely to be less alert and less fitted for strenuous resistance.

One night an attack was made on us, though it did not turn out to be anything very serious and was possibly simply a piece of bravado on the part of some of the young warriors who were anxious for war. They had not time to do much damage before we arrived on the scene and repulsed them, with the loss of a few killed.

Up to this time I had not really attached much importance to the rumours that an attack was to be made on us from that quarter, though I had taken all precautions against being caught napping.

I saw that it was necessary that we should be thoroughly prepared and set to work to make my plans accordingly. Crossing the country through which the enemy would have to come was a deep ravine with a river running through it. This river was crossed by a few bridges consisting simply of felled trees. I gave orders for these bridges to be destroyed, with the exception of one, over which I kept a guard night and day, to give us full warning of the enemy's coming. My intention was to destroy the bridge as soon as the opposing force had crossed it, in the hope that I might be able to teach them such a lesson that they would leave us alone for the future.

At the top of the mountain overlooking the ravine I had built another house for myself, with a food station, and trading store attached, and it was here that I decided to wait for the invaders. I had put a guard there, which I visited every day myself to see that things were all in order. The only path up the hill from the bridge zig-zagged up the mountain side, and was very rough and steep, so that it was difficult for an enemy to approach in a body.

The people living near this station were in continual fear of an attack, as they had news from their spies, that a considerable number of Masai were on the Kikuyu boundary, near Tato, and it has been the custom of this tribe to raid the country at least once a year, when the young braves would come out on the war-path to prove their fighting qualities. Their main object was loot, but they did not hesitate to kill all who opposed them, besides burning the villages and carrying off the cattle, and very often the women as well. I determined if possible to put an end to this raiding and wanton bloodshed.

The men guarding the bridge had been instructed to send two of their number to bring me word as soon as they saw the enemy approaching, while the remainder were to stay behind in hiding, and destroy the bridge as soon as the invaders had crossed.

The long expected attack came early one morning, and following out their instructions, the watchers at the bridge gave me early warning that a large body of warriors had crossed the river, and we were quite ready to give them a warm reception. They came boldly on, never thinking that we were waiting for them, and no doubt expecting the same easy victory that they had had on previous raids.

Owing to the narrowness of the path, they could only approach in single file, and we waited until they had almost reached the top before letting them know we were there. I had given strict orders that no man was to make a move, or utter a sound, until I gave the signal by firing my rifle. Coming steadily on, they had got close upon us when I fired, and my riflemen opened on them at once, while the bow-men followed the volley up with a flight of poisoned arrows. The invaders were taken completely by surprise, and before they could recover themselves the Kikuyu warriors swept down upon them with swords and spears. Bolting in a mad panic, they were hotly pursued down the mountain side, suffering severely in their flight. Arriving at the river, they found that the bridge was gone, and many of them jumped into the stream. Some got safely across, but a good many were drowned on the way. At least fifty had been killed, and many wounded. I gave orders that the wounded were not to be killed, but brought in as prisoners, of whom, when all were collected, we had a very large number, so that the victory was altogether complete, while my force had suffered only very slight loss.

The punishment we had administered was so severe that the country was never again raided by these people during the time I was with the Kikuyu.

This victory having ensured the people's security from any further raids (for a time, at any rate), I had now the opportunity for which I had been looking, of taking the food I had collected into the British Settlement. I had bought a lot of flour, which I took into the Government station at Naivasha, and very pleased they were to get it, as I found that they were practically starving. Not only was this the case at Naivasha, but they were no better off at the Ravine, and so thankful were the Government to get these supplies that they made a contract with me to keep them provisioned, and I heard no more about my going into the Kikuyu country without permission.

It appeared that during my absence from the Kikuyu country, my old partner, Gibbons, had returned from Uganda and gone into partnership with a man named Findlay, to make a trading expedition to the Kikuyu country; but I had somehow missed him while transacting my business in Naivasha, as his route had lain farther to the East.

I found that as soon as they had entered the country they had had trouble with the natives, and some of their men had been killed. They had taken with them forty or fifty armed men, with rifles, and about one hundred porters, intending to trade for ivory. So far as I could gather, a Chief had come to them and told them that he had a tusk to sell. When the Kikuyu come to sell ivory, they do not show you the tusk, but give you the measurement, from which you have to guess the weight; then, after the bargain is struck you pay for the ivory, and the seller is supposed to bring it in. Gibbons bought the tusk, and sent ten armed men back with the Chief to fetch it   These men were Swahili, who were terribly afiaid of the Kikuyu   They had received the ivory, and were bringing it back to camp, when they were all ambushed and murdered   The rest of the safari lost heart at the murder of their companions and had scarcely courage to defend themselves, and Gibbons saw that his only chance was to build a boma, as the natives were coming in force to attack him.   They had barely completed the boma. when they were attacked, and throughout the night the improvised fort was surrounded by a yelling horde of savages, bombarding them with spears and arrows, and trying by every means to get through the defences. Gibbons and Findlay kept up a plucky defence, and by spurring on their men managed to beat off the attack   Things, however, looked even worse in the morning, when the natives were reinforced, and hemmed them in on every side   It was impossible to remain in the boma, as they could not hope to hold it for long against the hundreds of black fiends who surrounded them, and it was decided to make a sortie and, if possible, cut their way through and get out of the country   The attempt was made, and a fierce hand-to-hand fight ensued, in which Findlay received two bad spear thrusts, and would have been killed outright, had not one of his boys come to the rescue, firing his rifle so close to Findlay's assailant that he blew his arm clean off   Findlay was carried back into the boma, to which Gibbons and the few survivors also returned, and then managed to strengthen their defences sufficiently to enable them to hold the savages at bay until a messenger got through to the nearest Government station, from which a relief force of the King's African Rifles was sent out, and after a week of terrible hardship Gibbons and his few remaining followers were rescued, Findlay, however, died later of his wounds.   This incident gives a good idea of the treacherous and blood-thirsty nature of the people among whom I was now spending my life

I was consolidating my position and getting my army better organised.   I could now within a day or so muster an army of some 5,000 men I had got into uniform and we looked a very formidable and smart lot, as we marched out with the Union Jack proudly floating at the head

I was now ready to extend my territory still further North, so one day, I set out with my body-guard and one hundred picked warriors, and after three days march, we arrived at the foot hill of Mount Kenya.   There I was met by all the big chiefs of the district, the most powerful being Wagombie   Another was named Karkerrie, who was Chief of Tato   A powerful witch-doctor also turned up, named Mugawa-Diga and last of all Olomondo, chief of the Wandarobo hunters   It was then arranged that I should make a blood-brotherhood with them all   The ceremony of blood-brother-hood was looked upon as a great event in the country, and the occasion for much feasting and rejoicing   Thousands of natives attended, each chief bringing a crowd of followers, while all the tribes in the neighbourhood were fully represented, but no women or children were present   Wagombie took quite a large number of his people, and I took the bulk of mine, leaving only a few in charge of the camp   An immense crowd had already gathered when we arrived. It was a stirring spectacle to see these thousands of warrior gathered together in their savage glory, their bodies elaborately painted and oiled, and each man armed with spear and shield, their dress of skins adding to their savage appearance.

The natives were for the most part standing about, but a few of the older men were sitting down talking the matter over, and our arrival was greeted with shouting and singing. I was naturally the centre of interest. I had the Union Jack with me as usual, and as we advanced there was a lull in the conversation and all became quiet and expectant.

Noticing that some had already begun drinking, I advised the chiefs that it would be much better to leave the drinking until their return to their homes, as having previously been hostile to each other, I was afraid that they would get drunk, and start to quarrel, which would spoil everything. The chiefs readily fell in with my suggestion, and at my suggestion also, all the weapons were placed on the ground, the warriors depositing their swords and shields in heaps, while four of my men were told off to guard.

When all the people were gathered round in a circle with the chief actors in the middle, I addressed them through an interpreter, and explained the object of the gathering, telling them that they were met together on friendly terms to make blood-brother-hood with the chiefs of the country, and that it was for this reason, that they had been asked to lay aside their weapons. While this was going on a fire had been lighted and a sheep was brought in and killed. Each Chief had supplemented what I had said with some words to the same effect, the old witch-doctor, Mugawa-Diga, being the most loquacious, and taking full advantage of the opportunity thus afforded him of indulging his vanity.

During the speechmaking the chiefs and myself were grouped round the fire talking together while the process of cooking certain parts of the sheep was going on. The heart and liver were taken out and cut into little pieces, which were then roasted separately on a skewer, carefully cut and shaved clean before the meat was put on.

When all the cooking was finished the orators ceased talking, and all the attention was turned on us. Olomondo, the chief hunter was the first to take a prominent part in the ceremony. Taking one of his sharp arrows he made an incision just above the heart in the flesh of each one who was to be joined in blood-brother-hood. When this had been done the meat was passed round, each one receiving a piece, which he first rubbed in the blood from the wound, made by the arrow, and then handed it to his neighbour who had already done the same with the meat he had received. The meat was then eaten, and this went on until each one had eaten the blood. This completed the ceremony and everyone turned to dancing and rejoicing, sheep and goats were killed and roasted and a big feast was held. During the feast I was informed by Wagombie that seven white men were on Mount Kenya, and they were after taking the mountain. He said he had already killed some of their people, and showed me a gun which he had taken from one of them, as I was the only white man they knew and now that I was a blood-brother of theirs, they wanted me to have the mountain and to make it legal according to native law, I had to give them some sheep, so I gave ten sheep to Wagombie, and ten to Olomondo, and that closed the bargain, and I became the proud possessor of Mount Kenya, the second biggest mountain in Africa

The Government, of course, will not recognise my claim. I brought the matter up before Sir Morrison Carter, Land Commissioner, in 1932, but without avail The seven white men who were on Mount Kenya at that time were Sir Alfred Mackinder's expedition

After the ceremony of blood-brother-hood, I went with my blood-brother Olomondo, chief of the Wandarobo hunters, on a hunting trip round my newly acquired mountain

After some weeks of good sport, I returned to the Kikuyu country and loaded up with ivory, I was very anxious to get back to my headquarters, as a rumour had spread through the country that I had been killed Just after leaving Tato, the rumour reached me that three Goanese had been murdered and their safari wiped out. I gathered that it was a trading safari which had started out from Nairobi They had entered the Kikuyu country, and had been well-treated by the natives, and had had a good time until they had entered the Chinga country These were the only natives I had never really got in touch with We had passed through their country just after leaving Karuri's and for the most part they had kept out of my way The Goanese, having had a good time at Karuri's, had, perhaps, not reckoned on the other natives being different, and consequntly had not taken proper precautions They were well-armed—about fifteen of the natives carrying rifles, besides themselves—but in spite of this, the Chingas had attacked them and murdered the whole party

This was the disquieting rumour that reached me soon after leaving Tato, though I must confess that I did not put much faith in it, as so many similar rumours had been spread about myself having been killed, and I had learned not to trust every report that I heard. I thought, however, that the Goanese might be in some difficulty, and perhaps had some of their men killed, so I hurried up to see if I could give them any assistance; but the nearer I got, the more convincing were the statements of the natives, as to the truth of the stories which I had heard

I did not call at Muga-wa-Diga's as I had done on my outward journey, but took the shorter route to Bartier's, and when nearing his village did a very foolish thing, which might have easily cost me my life, and, indeed, probably would have done so, but for the extraordinary instinct of my mule

Being anxious to meet Bartier, to get confirmation of the statements I had heard from the natives and as it was getting late in the afternoon, I left my men and hurried on ahead I had never done such a thing before, but it must be remembered that I was carrying with me an immense quantity of ivory—practically every man being fully loaded with it—and my anxiety about the Goanese had shaken me out of my usual caution Taking with me only one askari, my gunbearer, an interpreter and the boy who looked after my mule, I went on, telling the rest to follow me as quickly as possible to Bartier's. My men knew what had happened, and I told them to be very careful; but still; being in a friendly country, I thought that there could be no harm in pushing ahead by myself. The path ran between two hedges, which separated it on either side from the cultivated patches of the natives.

Suddenly, as I galloped forward, my mule showed a disinclination to proceed along the path, and seemed to want to get off the road into the cultivated patches. This curious behaviour would at any other time have roused my suspicions, but though puzzled to account for the mule's peculiar conduct, I did not attach any special reason to it, and finding that it would not go along the path, I let it have its own way, and turned into the shamba, when it ran along without any further trouble.

I galloped along for some distance, near the footpath, and had not gone more than a mile when the mule of its own accord, returned to the road, and I arrived at Bartier's without further incident about five o'clock.

The whole village was in a state of excitement, and I quickly received confirmation of the murders, the natives being full of it, and, appearing terribly afraid that Chinga people would attack them immediately because I was there. The Chinga people were their neighbours, and the Goanese who had been murdered being white men, were said to be my brothers. Hitherto many of the natives had believed that it was impossible to kill a white man, and this idea had, to a great extent, kept me free from attack. But now they said that they had killed my brothers, and were only waiting for an opportunity to kill me as well.

Bartier and his people assured me that they were absolutely friendly to me, and that I could rely on them. It was the Chinga people, with the natives from a place called Mahigga, together with some from a district lying more to the East of us, under the control of my old enemy, the chief-rain-maker, who had joined their forces against the Goanese, and I had no doubt that the rain-maker had had as much, and more to do with the matter than anyone else. From what I could make out there must have been some thousands of natives in the business, and they had completely wiped out the trader's safari and taken everything they possessed—trade goods, some cattle they had with them, and everything that was worth looting.

While Bartier was explaining all this to me, two of the four men who had started out with me ahead of the main body of my followers arrived in the village. I had out-distanced them on my mule, and had been feeling some anxiety for their safety. When I saw that there were only two of them, I enquired what had become of the others. It was evident from the state of excitement they were in that something had happened, and they told me that two of their companions had been killed. Their story confirmed the suspicion which had been growing in my mind, that an ambush had been set for me at the place where my mule had refused to keep on the road, and it was no doubt due to the animal's instinct that I had not been killed, as my men had kept to the road and so fallen into the ambush. They were going along, they said, when a number of men rushed out on them, and before they knew what was really happening two of the number had been killed. The two men who had escaped could only tell me that they had been attacked by a number of Kikuyu on the war-path, who, rushing out on them had speared the others and then cleared off, while they had picked up the rifles of the murdered men and come on to Bartier's as fast as they could. I saw that things were looking pretty bad, and quickly concluded that the men in ambush were some of the party who had taken part in the murder of the Goanese, but whether they were merely a scouting party spying out my movements who had got a bit excited and started too early, or whether they had planned to kill me and throw suspicion on Bartier, I could only guess. Bartier assured me that it had not been done by any of his people and I was quite prepared to believe him, being fully convinced in my own mind that it was the act of some of the Chinga people.

As soon as I had gathered all the details from my two followers I asked Bartier to send out a few of his people to meet my caravan, to tell them what had happened and to warn them to be careful; also, if the two men who had been ambushed were not dead, to bring them in with them, and this he readily agreed to do. My men were not very far behind, and the caravan shortly afterwards arrived, bringing with them one of the men still alive. He had had two or three spears thrust through his back. I did all I possibly could for him but he was past human help, and, after confirming the story which the others had already told me, he died in an hour or two.

As soon as the caravan arrived we at once set to work to build a boma, and I realised that I was now in about the tightest corner I had ever been in. With all these men of the Goanese safari murdered the country was in a state of ferment and thousands of men armed on the war-path all around us, so that the prospect was not cheerful, and I could see that I was in for a rough time, and how I was going to get out of it I could not imagine.

As I have said, I had such an amount of ivory that I could only just get along and I was not disposed to abandon it, after all the months of trouble and worry it had cost me to collect, living entirely among savages, and never seeing a white face for twelve months. At any rate, I meant to make a good fight for it and determined if it were at all possible, to win my way out though I knew all these people who had already dipped their hands in the blood of my white brothers—as they imagined them to be—would do their utmost to blot me out, if only for the sake of the quantity of loot which they would expect to get.

The next step to building a boma was to bury the ivory, and make this as secure as possible. It was soon evident that information of our arrival had spread through the hostile tribes, whose war-cries could be heard on every side, while bands of warriors could be seen gathering all round us, and the whole country was soon alive with armed natives yelling their war-cries. Having had a comparatively easy victory over the Goanese they confidently expected to dispose of me without very much trouble. Some of the natives had dressed themselves in the clothes of the Goanese and proudly paraded themselves in front of my camp, whilst others were firing off the guns they had taken. For the time being, however, they kept at a respectful distance and we went on strengthening our defences; but it made my blood boil when I saw that they had cut off the heads of the murdered men and stuck them on poles, which they were carrying about as trophies. I knew what my fate would be, if I were unlucky enough to fall into their clutches, while my anxiety was increased by the fact that our stock of ammunition was running very low.

As far as I could learn, the Chinga people could muster about five thousand fighting men, reckoning in other tribes who were standing in with them, and the only course open to me was to stand on the defensive.

Bartier promised to give me all the help he could, but I could see that his people were terribly afraid, and I could understand their feeling, as, if they befriended me, and it should happen that the Chinga people wiped me out, then they would be in for it. Bartier did, however, give me all the information he could, and assisted me as much as I could reasonably expect under the circumstances. At the same time, I could see that he was badly frightened, which, perhaps, was only natural, seeing that the other side were so strong, and seemed quite determined to carry things to the bitter end. They had already commenced hostilities by murdering my two men, and, fired by their success in wiping out the other safari, were burning to get at me.

Since the wholesale murder of the Goanese and their followers, they had been rejoicing and feasting and drinking a lot of njohi, and now they were dancing about in paroxysms of mad fury, all alike being possessed with the war fever and ready at any moment to break loose upon us, while we could only wait their first move and take every precaution we could think of.

We were camping right on the boundary of the two countries, and could plainly hear them shouting, so I sent some of Bartier's men, with some of my own, to scout, with orders to hang about in the bush and in the shamba and try and find out what the plans of the enemy were.

At midnight news was brought in that a large force of natives was gathered in one of the clearings about a mile from the camp, where they usually held their war-dances, and were drinking and feasting and discussing how they should attack us. This threw all the people about us into a state of panic, expecting every minute that the crowd assembling in the clearing would be rushing down on us, though I knew that this would be a most unusual thing for them to do, as savages very rarely rush a camp at night, usually reserving their attack till dawn; still, having had success before, and having been drinking, I thought that there was a reasonable possibility that they might depart from their usual rule on this occasion. Of course, sleep was out of the question, and everybody had to stand to arms.

A large number of Bartier's people were in my camp and everyone was in a nervous state of expectancy. Eventually, a dead silence reigned, the effect of which, when surrounded by a host of armed foes, I have endeavoured to describe before. I had experienced the same feeling during the night we were surrounded by the natives at Tato. The feeling of depression was almost unbearable, and was not lessened by the lonesomeness of my position, out in the midst of a wild country, far removed from any white men, waiting in momentary expectation of the rush of a horde of yelling savages thirsting for blood—and loot—of the white man who had so far defied all attempts to blot him out, and seemed only to gain fresh power in the country after every attempt that was made against him. The situation was nerve-trying in the extreme, and after an hour or so of waiting in this horrible silence, I wanted to shout in sheer desperation or do anything rather than endure the inactivity any longer.

I felt the responsibility for the safety of the followers I had brought into this position and the risk of losing the whole fruits of my twelve months' trying experiences, and could not sit still, but had to keep moving about. Even the movement did not serve to relieve the tension, and I felt that if I did not do something quickly I should be getting hysterical, so I quickly decided to put into action an idea which had been gradually forming in my brain of giving my friends, the enemy, a surprise, instead of waiting for them to give me one. I at once gave orders for big fires to be made up and for everything to be done which would give the camp the appearance of being occupied by the whole of my force and then, leaving only a few men in charge of the camp, I mustered the remainder and stole quietly out, my men being fully armed, to pay a visit to a place in the clearing where the enemy were said to be holding a consultation—my object being to teach them such a lesson that they would hesitate to make war on me again.

The enemy evidently had never imagined that we should venture to turn the tables on them in this manner, and in the darkness we managed to creep right up to the edge of the clearing without being discovered, as they had not thought it necessary to put sentries out. Here we found the warriors still drinking and feasting, sitting round their fires so engrossed in their plans for my downfall that they entirely failed to notice our approach; so, steadily creeping up till we were close behind them, we prepared to complete our surprise. The moment had come to deal them a crushing blow.

Not a sound betrayed our advance, and they were still quite ignorant of our presence. The crack of my rifle, which was the signal for the general attack, was immediately drowned in the roar of the other guns as my men poured a volley which could not fail to be effective at that short range, while accompanying the leaden missiles was a cloud of arrows, poured in by that part of my force that was not armed with rifles.

The effect of this unexpected onslaught was electrical, the savages starting up with yells of terror in a state of utter panic. Being taken so completely by surprise, they could not at first realise what had happened, and the place was for a few minutes a pandemonium of howling natives, who rushed about in the faint light of the camp fires, jostling each other and stumbling over the bodies of those who had fallen at the first volley, but quite unable to see who had attacked them; while, before they had recovered from the first shock of surprise, my men had re-loaded, and again a shower of bullets and arrows carried death into the seething, disorganised mass. This volley completed the rout, and, without waiting a moment longer, the whole crowd rushed pell-mell into the bush, not a savage remaining in the clearance that could get away, and the victory was complete.

For the time being we were masters of the situation, only a number of still forms and a few wounded being left of the thousands who had filled the clearing a little while before, and we returned jubilant to our camp.

As may be imagined, our success was a great relief to me, and I reckoned that I had taught them a lesson, which would make them hesitate before interfering with me again; so, leaving my buried ivory, I started off the next morning, in an attempt to get through to my headquarters, feeling sure that Karuri must by this time have heard of my position, and would send out a force to meet me.

Our advance was made with the utmost caution; halting every few minutes to search with our eyes the scrub on either side of the path for any sign of a lurking foe, and keeping our guns ready to fire at the sight of an enemy, we went slowly on until we entered the Chinga country.

Skirting the edge of one of the hills, our way led through a large patch of thick grass, some seven or eight feet high—an ideal place for an ambush—and I felt that if we got safely through this there was little else to fear. Step by step we proceeded, going dead slow, and making scarcely a sound, but we had not gone far before we instinctively felt that our enemies were hidden in the long grass around us, and our suspicious were soon confirmed.

A black form was seen for a second, and then instantly disappeared. Then shots were fired, and spears and arrows began to whizz about our heads, and before we had gone many yards farther, the grass around us became alive with savages. Whenever one showed himself, we fired, and then suddenly the grass became animated on all sides, swayed and parted, and the horde of yelling, black demons were upon us.

We were fighting at close quarters, and very soon every man had his work cut out to defend himself. I was loading and firing from the hip, as fast as I could throw out the empty shells, and push fresh cartridges into the breech. It was a critical moment, and it looked very much as though it was all up with us.

So closely were we being pressed that one of the savages had his spear poised over my head, and the muzzle of my rifle was pressed against his body when I fired. My first shot seemed to paralyse him, for while he had plenty of time to plunge his spear into my body he failed to do so, and I plumped two or three bullets into him before he jumped into the air, and toppled over dead.

My followers were all equally hard pressed, and on all sides was a writhing mass of black forms, all fighting like devils. We were in a valley, closed in by rugged hills, and chancing to look up, I saw that the top of the mountain above us was black with natives, who were evidently only waiting to see how those below fared before making a final rush, which must have swamped us; so I immediately shouted to my men to rush up the hill, thinking that if we waited much longer they might suddenly decide to sweep down on us, when our last chance of getting away would be gone.

We had by this time stopped the rush of those in the valley, and now, taking the offensive, we fought our way through them, up the mountain side; but when the force on the top saw us coming, they at once turned and bolted, rushing helter-skelter down the other side of the hill.

We had had a marvellous escape, and though we had had several casualties, we had come out of the affair with much smaller loss than might have been expected.

I saw that it was useless to try to get through to Karuri's now, as we should have to fight every foot of the way, and had practically no chance of winning through; so we returned to Bartier's.

By this time the news had spread through the country, and Wagombi and Karkerrie had heard of my trouble, and had sent some men to help me, with a promise of more if I needed them.

The whole country was thrown into a state of excitement; the war fever was at its height; but my blood-brothers had rallied nobly to my help, and big forces of armed warriors were coming in every hour from the different chiefs to support me, until I had a force of several thousands of the finest fighting men in the country camped at Bartier's.

I was considerably alarmed at the turn events had taken, especially as the chiefs were determined to have it out, and threatened to clean up the whole Chinga country; while the hostile natives had, in the meantime, collected more followers, having received reinforcements from some of the other tribes living to the East, so that I could see that it was absolutely useless to try to make peace until they had had a tussle.

The people who had come to help me were also red-hot for war, and scenes of the wildest enthusiasm prevailed in the camp of my force. Giving way to their savage nature, they danced themselves into the wildest passion, numbers of them going into hysterical fits, and jabbing their spears into tree-trunks in imitation of killing their enemies, while their breath sobbed out in great gulps. It was a remarkable outburst of savage uncontrolled passion which I was helpless to check.

When the time for action came, this army of warriors swept through the Chinga country from one end to the other, destroying the villages and wiping out of existence all who had opposed them. It was some time before peace could be restored, and when that time came, the Chinga people, as a force to be reckoned with in the country, had ceased to exist.

The trouble being thus settled, I got my ivory through to headquarters, being met on the road by Karuri, bringing a force to my assistance, my messengers having acquainted him with the state of affairs.

From this time on I had complete control of the country; everything that had been stolen from the Goanese was given up, while their murderers had received punishment they were not likely to forget for a generation.

When matters had quietened down again and I had time to review the situation, I took the first opportunity of sending messengers through to the Government, with a full report of the recent occurrences; while I also communicated with the relatives of the murdered Goanese, two brothers, who, I heard, were living at Nairobi, sending through to them the whole of the stolen property which I had recovered. I found out later, that through a misunderstanding, the heads of the murdered men—which had been found after the fighting was over—had likewise been sent to Nairobi; which, while serving as proof to the officials that the reports I had been sending in from time to time as to the character of the natives were not without foundation, was a most regrettable occurrence, and must, I fear, have given much pain to the relatives.

The fighting being now over, and the Chinga people—such as remainded of them—having given assurances of their desire and intention to live at peace with their neighbours, the country now settled down to a condition of quietness such as had never been known before. My mission through the country had served to produce a spirit of friendship between the different clans and tribes which effectively put an end to the petty quarrelling and constant fighting which had hitherto gone on. From this time I was looked upon as practically the king of the country, all matters in dispute being referred to my judgment and I was constantly being called upon to give counsel and advice upon every conceivable subject which affected the welfare of the people. The three most powerful chiefs in the country, Karuri, Karkerrie, and Wagombi, acknowledged me as their leader, and chiefs and people were now entirely under my control. As proof of the altered condition of the country, I could now send messengers to any one of the chiefs or headmen without any fear of their being attacked or molested on the way.

It was about this time that smallpox broke out in the country and for the time being all my other troubles were relegated to the background in the face of the necessity for dealing with this awful plague.

We were having a shauri, when I noticed in the crowd an elderly man, a stranger to that part of the country and a single glance was sufficient to show me that he was suffering from smallpox. I explained to the natives the significance of my discovery, and told them that if he were allowed to mix with them they would certainly get the disease and die. They immediately stood away from him and said that I ought to shoot him, which to their savage minds was the most natural precaution to prevent the disease spreading. I explained to them that such a course was impossible, though in view of the subsequent events, the forfeiture of this man's life at that time would have meant the saving of thousands of lives which were lost in the epidemic of which he was the cause. I told the natives what they ought to do to avoid the infection, and arranged for an isolation camp to be built in which the man was placed, telling some of the people who lived near to leave food for him at a reasonable distance, so that he could fetch it for himself until he got better, and also instructed them to see that he did not, on any account, leave the camp.

Some days later I was travelling through the country when I again saw the man in the crowd, and in great alarm sent some of my men back to the isolation camp with him. But it was too late The disease had already spread to others, and I saw a lot of bad cases among the people, and though I tried to get them all into isolation camps, it was impossible. When an outbreak occurred in a family they would not report it, but continued to live and sleep together in the same hut, with the result that, in most cases, the whole family took the disease and died.

I sent to Naivasha for some lymph and started vaccinating the people. They took the matter in the proper light, and raised no objection, so that I was able to vaccinate thousands of them, which must, undoubtedly, have been the means of saving many lives; but in spite of all I could do, thousands died, many whole villages being wiped out.

One rather remarkable thing about this epidemic was that Karuri's village escaped entirely, not a single case occurring among the inhabitants, which Karuri claimed to be due to certain precautions he took to ward off the evil. He got some sticks and split them down the middle, and then poured some black powder in the opening, afterwards pegging the sticks down across all the footpaths leading to the village. It did not keep people from coming in, and I could not see in what way the sticks could do any good, but Karuri had great faith in their virtues, and as no case of smallpox occurred in the village, he took the credit for keeping it away.

The failure of the rains for two successive seasons — which was attributed to the white man having brought the railway into the country—brought about a famine which still further depleted the population.

The country around Karuri's, being mountainous, was not affected so much as the part to the east of us, on the caravan road, and more towards the coast. At our high elevation, surrounded by the water-sheds of Mount Kenia and the Aberdare Range, we could always rely on a fair amount of rain, though we had had much less than usual during these two seasons. The general famine in the country affected me, inasmuch as the food which I was there to buy found its way out on the borders of the country, and consequently my supplies were cut off. Having occasion to go down to Nairobi about this time, I saw hundreds of poor wretches dead or dying on the road, while some of my men heard gruesome tales of men killing and eating each other in their desperation at the lack of food. No case of this kind came under my personal notice, but I have seen the natives sitting down and boiling the skins which they wore as clothing in the effort to soften them sufficiently to enable them to be eaten.

Numbers of the starving people, when they heard that food was to be got in the part of the country from which I came, started out to try to get there, but were robbed and killed on the way by the Kalyera people. It sounds rather paradoxical speaking of starving people being robbed, but the statement is nevertheless perfectly true, and, before starting out, these poor vagrants collected all their household goods and took them along with them, in the hope of exchanging them for food. Thousands of these people would start off together and being weak and exhausted with hunger, they fell an easy prey to the Kalyera.

The natives begged me to take them out to Karuri's, and pitying their miserable condition, I agreed to do so, and got together a caravan of several thousands of the starving wretches, among whom were a number of natives who possessed a fair quantity of sheep—perhaps one man would have thirty sheep, and another five or six heads of cattle, while, of course, there were numbers of others who had absolutely nothing. It was pitiable to see these people staggering along first one and then another dropped out to die on the road. Before starting out I made it perfectly plain to them that I would only lead them to the " Land of Promise " on condition that they placed themselves absolutely under my control and obeyed my orders in everything, and this they promised to do. When I saw them staggering along, almost too weak to drag one foot before the other, and dying at the rate of about fifty a day, I ordered those who had cattle and sheep to deliver them up to me, and each night when we got into camp, I had as many killed as were required to give them just enough to keep them alive. I got thousands of these starving people to my headquarters, where I was able to feed them, thereby saving some thousands of lives.

I had been living and trading in the Kikuyu country for something like two-and-a-half years now, and during that time had had no white visitors in the country, when one day the news was brought in that some white men had come into my neighbourhood. News of an event of this sort, of course, spreads very quickly and the natives reported to me that at Mberri, about thirty miles to the east of my headquarters, two white men were camping with a lot of troops, and had commenced to build a fort. When I made a few enquiries I found that they were Government officials, who had come out to take over the country, and when I was satisfied of this, as soon as I could spare the time, I called all the chiefs together and told them that these two white men were evidently officers of the Government and had come to take the country over, and that as it had hitherto fallen to my lot to settle quarrels and disputes and generally manage the affairs of the whole country, so now, I explained, these newcomers had been sent for that purpose, and to take my place. I gave the chiefs some days notice to be ready to go up with me, and said that I would take them up and introduce them to the officials.

When the time came to start for Mberri, all the chiefs did not turn up, but I found that a good number of the thirty-six who at that time looked to me as their head were ready to accompany me. Each chief brought some of his followers with him, and we started off with about one thousand men, and, as it was too far for a day's march ,I camped after travelling about three-parts of the way to the fort. Resuming our journey the next morning, we had nearly covered the remaining portion of the distance, when it suddenly struck me that if such a large body of armed natives were seen approaching the fort without any notice of their coming having been received, they might easily be mistaken for a hostile force coming to attack the new station, so I called a halt, two or three miles from the fort, and, leaving the natives behind, went on ahead to report their arrival.

On reaching Mberri I met one of the officers in charge of the fort ,who turned out to be Mr. F. G. Hall. I had previously met him at Fort Smith when he was in charge of that station. The other was also known to me through my having been in communication with him on several occasions respecting certain happenings in the Kikuyu country.

The two officials received me in a friendly way and invited me to have breakfast with them. Having reported to them that I had brought in a number of friendly chiefs to introduce to them, and explained my mission, I sent a man back to tell my people to come in, and was still at breakfast when I heard a lot of shouting and talking and went out to see what was the matter. I was told that my askaris were being placed under arrest as they had no right to be in uniform. As a matter of fact, they were not wearing a Government uniform, but as they were all dressed alike in khaki, this was made a ground for interference and the officer proceeded to cut some buttons off their tunics, and the rank badges off the arms of the sergeant and corporal. I had previously ordered my men to disarm, and they submitted very quietly to this disfigurement of their clothes. My chief offence, however, was the fact that I was flying the Union Jack, which my men carried with them, as they were accustomed to do on all their expeditions. I mildly put the question to the officer as to whether he expected me to fly the Russian flag, or any other, except that of my own country, but it seemed that it was a most serious offence for an Englishman to display the flag unless he held some position in the official oligarchy of the country.

In the meantime, a fearful row was going on amongst my people and the other Kikuyu who lived near Mberri, who had joined them. The officers asked me why I had brought all these men there, saying there was bound to be a fight and no end of trouble. I told them that there would be no trouble with my men as I could manage them alright. They asked me to disarm them, and I agreed to do so, provided that they would be responsible for their weapons, and on their undertaking to do so, I explained to the chiefs that it was the white man's wish that they should disarm. This they very reluctantly consented to do, and gave up their weapons on my assuring them that they would be restored to them. When my men were all disarmed, and their weapons had been safely stowed away in a tent, under the care of a sentry, the official announced that I was to consider myself a prisoner as well.

To this I merely replied, " All right," thinking that if I expressed the annoyance and resentment which I felt, it would only lead to more unpleasantness and possible trouble. I was told that I should be able to retain my cook and personal servants, and that no restraint would be put upon my movements, provided I would give my word of honour not to attempt to clear out.

As my real offence was that I had brought into a state of order a country which, previous to my coming, had such a reputation that no official would set foot across the border if he could help it, I had no cause to fear the results of an investigation in my conduct, and I made up my mind to await calmly the termination of this comedy. Besides, I thought that my personal influence might very likely be needed to prevent some " regrettable occurrence." Both the officials were uncertain as to what the natives might do and any hasty or foolish act might easily have set the whole country in a blaze. So I retired to my tent and amused myself for a great part of the day with a gramophone which I had brought with me. Of course, my men could not understand what had happened, and fortunately, none of them knew that I was under arrest.

In the meantime they were being questioned as to what had happened in the Kikuyu country during the time that I had been there; and the following day an askari came to my tent and presented me with a lengthy document, written on blue paper, which proved to be a summons to appear that day before the officers in charge of the fort.

The summons read somewhat as follows:—

" I charge you, John Boyes, that during your residence in the Kenia district, you waged war, set shauris, personated Government, went on six punitive expeditions, and committed dacoity."

I must confess that I read over this formidable list of charges with some amusement, though I was well aware that any one of them, if proved, meant capital punishment. There was one item on the list that I could not make out, and I took the first opportunity of enquiring the meaning of the word " dacoity," which was a term I had never heard used in the country before.

I remembered reading a book called, " The Last of the Dacoits," and it struck me that either the title of the book was wrong, or that the official, in his anxiety to fulfil his instructions to pile up as heavy a list of crimes against me as possible, had allowed his imagination to run away with him. It was explained to me that " Dacoit " was an Indian term, meaning a native outlaw.

At the time appointed I presented myself at the " Court House," which was a primitively constructed mud-hut, furnished with two chairs and a table, and as the two former were occupied by the officers, there was nothing for me but to make myself as comfortable as possible on the corner of the table, which I did, much to their indignation. The charge having been read over to me, I was cautioned in the same manner as an English bobby cautions a prisoner, that anything I might say, etc., and then I was asked what I had to say. I told them that I certainly had nothing to say to them one way or the other, and would reserve my defence, and the proceedings —which were of a purely formal character—were then over, and I returned to my tent

The next four days were spent in collecting evidence against me and as nobody could be persuaded to go to my headquarters to collect evidence on the spot, the soldier finally went, taking with him the whole of his troops, while during his absence the civilian guard gathered all the information he could from the chiefs and other natives at Mberri

When they had, as they thought, obtained sufficient evidence to secure my conviction, the Kikuyu who had come in with me had their arms restored to them, and I and my personal body-guard, together with about two hundred native witnesses, were sent down to Nairobi under charge of an escort of about ten native soldiers, commanded by a black sergeant ! The situation was ludicrously Gilbertian. Here was I, a (so-called) dangerous outlaw, being sent down to be tried for my life on a series of serious indictments, through a country in which I had only to lift my little finger to call an army of savage warriors to my assistance I was accompanied by a personal following twenty times as numerous as the guard of ten natives who kept me prisoner, and who trembled every time they passed a native village lest the inhabitants should rush and wipe them out of existence, while on the first day out the humour of the situation was considerably increased by the sergeant in charge of the escort handing me the big blue envelope containing the statement of the evidence against me, with a request that I would take charge of it for him, as he was afraid he might lose it ' I must say that I thoroughly appreciated the humour of the whole affair I was the only mounted man in the whole outfit, still having my mule, and it struck me as distinctly amusing that I should be practically taking myself down to Nairobi to be tried for my life, with the whole of the evidence under my arm

When we arrived in Nairobi, I presented myself at the Government headquarters, which were then in a little tiny shanty, the remainder of the party sat down outside whilst I went in to see the official.

The Goanese clerk who enquired my business told me that the Sub-Commissioner was very busy just then and that I could not see him I had always experienced the same difficulty in getting an interview and no doubt the clerk thought that I had come to make one of my usual complaints. On this occasion I did not happen to be in a hurry, so telling the clerk that I would call back in about an hour's time I went for a stroll round the town On my return I was received by the Sub-Commissioner who asked me what I wanted, so I handed him the packet containing the statement of evidence, and when he looked through it, he said that he would make arrangements at once to have me sent down to Mombasa.

Things were done in a different way here, and I quickly realised the change when I got outside the office and found myself surrounded by a guard of six Indian soldiers with fixed bayonets. The same day I was taken by the afternoon train to Mombasa under charge of the escort of Indian soldiers with a white officer in command and on arriving there I was handed over to another white official. After some considerable delay, the papers apparently not being in order in some respect, I was duly admitted to Mombasa jail, which was the old Portuguese Fort.

Some weeks later I was tried at Nairobi, the Government having 400 witnesses against me, but all the witnesses spoke in my favour and I left the Court, as the Judge said, without a stain on my character, the Judge even going so far as to say that he did not understand why the case had been brought at all, and finally, apologised to me for the waste of my time.

After the fiasco of my trial, I returned to Karuri's and continued my food-buying, taking the supplies into Naivasha as before. I still experienced the same trouble with the Kalyera natives on the way down with the food for the Government stations, and finally the matter was reported to the Governor, Sir Charles Eliot, who resided at Zanzibar, which was then the headquarters of the Government. As a result of these representations, an expedition was sent out under Captain Wake, of the East African Rifles, with Mr. McLellan as civil officer, and I was asked to accompany them as a guide and intelligence officer. I was only too pleased to have this opportunity of proving to the Government my readiness to help, and willingly agreed to go with the expedition. After the expedition, Captain Wake sent me the following letter:—

Naivasha,
June 24th, 1901.

From Captain C. St. A. Wake, C.H.G., D.S.O.,
  East African Rifles.

Mr. John Boyes.

Sir,—Before leaving this station for the East African Protectorate, I wish to place on record the sense I entertain of the very valuable services rendered to the force under my command during the late Kalyera Punitive Expedition.

That you were able to render these services I attribute in a great measure to your tact and fair dealing with the Chief Karuri's people, and I shall not fail to bring to the notice of the Military Authorities in East Africa your very useful work during the last seven weeks.

I am, Sir,
Your obedient servant,
C. ST. A. WAKE,
Captain, E.A. Rifles,
Commdg. late
Kalyera Punitive Expedition.

After this **expedition** was over I found that the Governor, Sir Charles Eliot, had arrived in Nairobi; through the influence of Captain Wake I was able to meet him.

Some time later he asked me to arrange a safari, saying, " I should like you to show me your country," so I engaged porters and took him to Mberri, where we were met by practically all my old chiefs, and handed the whole country over to him.

After bidding good-bye to the Governor, I returned to my headquarters at Karuri's. Finding my pioneer work was over, I handed my headquarters over to some missionaries.

THE END.

www.ingramcontent.com/pod-product-compliance
Lightning Source LLC
Chambersburg PA
CBHW061105050726
47592CB00004B/1840